Mark Twain

In His Footsteps

Mark Twain In His Footsteps

by Ginny Benson
illustrated by Harold Henriksen

Creative Education
Mankato, Minnesota 56001

Published by Creative Education, 123 South Broad Street,
P. O. Box 227, Mankato, Minnesota 56001
Copyright © 1974 by Creative Education. No part of this book may be reproduced
in any form without written permission from the publisher. International copyrights
reserved in all countries. Printed in the United States.
Distributed by Childrens Press. 1224 West Van Buren Street, Chicago, Illinois 60607
Library of Congress Numbers: 74-2105   ISBN: 0-87191-325-9

Library of Congress Cataloging in Publication Data
Benson, Ginny, 1923
Mark Twain; In his footsteps.
(Personal close ups)
SUMMARY: A brief biography of the well-known nineteenth-century
author of "Tom Sawyer" and "Huckleberry Finn."
1. Clemens, Samuel Langhorne, 1835-1910—Biography—Juvenile literature.
[1. Clemens, Samuel Langhorne, 1835-1910. 2. Authors, American]
I. Henriksen, Harold, illus. II. Title.
PS1331.B4   818'.4'09 [B] [92]   74-2105   ISBN 0-87191-325-9

INTRODUCTION

Mark Twain was born just after Halley's comet had passed over Florida, Missouri. His family knew that he would somehow be special. From the time he was a small boy he had a way with words and could make anyone laugh. His mother once said he could make even a wooden Indian laugh.

This book takes us back through history to the time when Mark Twain was alive. We become reporters following his antics from the time he moved with his mother and father, his brothers — Orion, Henry, and Benjamin — and his sister Pamela to Hannibal, Missouri, on the Mississippi River until he was a grown man with a family of his own.

Travelling through his lifetime, we meet the people that he wrote about in his books and stories. We meet the characters that become Huckleberry Finn, Tom Sawyer, and Captain Stormfield. We learn how a young boy whose name was Samuel Clemens and who never finished grade school grew up to become the famous American author Mark Twain.

Dedicated to my son Robert Franklin Child III

Mark Twain In His Footsteps

When a boy of twelve is forced to leave school and ends up fifty years later with honorary degrees from big universities, somewhere between lies a strange and powerful story. Such is the life story of Samuel Langhorne Clemens, for nearly a half century known and celebrated as Mark Twain.

What fun it would be if we could turn back the pages of time and follow in his footsteps along that marvelous adventure that made him far more colorful than any of the

characters he created in his many books. How could he write so beautifully of the America of his day? Are you curious?

Let's pretend that we're roving reporters from today, hired by a big newspaper to get the Mark Twain story. We've been warned that we. have to stick to facts, report the truth and not exaggerate too much. Yet, in our excitement, we might borrow on our imaginations just a bit. After all, that's what all good feature writers do . . . even Mark Twain did it.

So sharpen your pencils, bring along your notebook, and pack a couple of peanut butter sandwiches if you like. Come with me to another time and place.

The sheets on the calendar are caught in the wind blowing us backward in time . . . back . . . back . . . back to the unhurried America of 1839, to a little village called Florida, hardly big enough to deserve a dot on the map of Missouri.

Here we are, walking along the dusty dirt road of this sleepy little town. Scattered log houses dot the landscape, surely no more than twenty of them in all. An old hound dog looks up from his afternoon snooze as we stroll by. There seems to be some activity down the road. A large wagon is being loaded with trunks and various household goods while neighbors stand around and watch.

"Hey there!" I call to one of the men. "What's going on?"

"Howdy, stranger! Well, sir, this here wagon is takin'

Mr. Clemens and his family to Hannibal 'bout fifty miles from here," he replies helpfully.

"Who is that black girl with the red bandana on her head, the one holding the hand of that wriggly child?"

"That's Jennie, the Clemens' slave gal. She takes care of that scallywag. He's little Sammy Clemens."

"Thanks," I say as we make our way up to Jennie and the youngster.

She is having a time with the child, keeping him out of the way while the rest of the family packs the wagon. We can see a young girl of about twelve with a box full of kittens, and a boy of fourteen helping his father move a treasured bureau. Another lad, maybe seven, has already climbed into the wagon to look on.

"I beg your pardon, Miss, but can I speak with you, Jennie?" I say, hoping I won't startle the young girl.

She turns and smiles at us and clutches the four-year-old boy closer to her. He is a thin, frail-looking lad with pale skin, a little too delicate to be healthy; but he tugs at Jennie's hand to be free with surprising energy. His blue-gray eyes dance with excitement as he breaks away and runs toward us.

"Hi there!" he says as if he recognized us.

"Sammy!" calls Jennie, clutching the back of his shirt. "Honestly dis chile is a wiggle-worm if'n thar evah was one!"

"He's quite a handful, isn't he?" I say.

"Dat he is! He's a special one, you know. Why, he can

tickle a smile into a laugh like no one else. Jus' two weeks 'fore he was born, a comet streaked across the sky. Folks called it Halley's Comet, but ah knows it was an omen dat dis fifth chile was gonna be special. He was born early, too. Everybody thought he was gonna die, so puny and sickly he was. But ah knew he wasn't. So did his Mammy. 'Course, he gave us a time what with catchin' every bug in sight. Measles! Mumps! Chicken pox! You name it, he had it! Guess he's a mite spoiled from all de fussin' and 'tention

he's had." Jennie looks at the boy lovingly.

"When his younger brother, Henry, was born 'bout a year ago, his nose fairly went out of joint," she continues. "De only thing dat helped was mah 'Once 'pon a time' stories. Sammy loves dem stories!"

"What kind does he like the best?" I ask.

"Well, ghost stories mostly. De ones 'bout shadows and spooks. His eyes get so big, and he screams with delight when ah pounces on him with a GOTCHA!" Jennie laughs happily remembering those fine times.

"Why is the family moving to Hannibal, Jennie?" I say.

"Cause Massah Clemens done been trained as a lawyer, and der just ain't much chance for him to make a livin' doin' dat here. Besides, he runs de dry goods store with his brother-in-law, John Quarles; but even dat ain't 'nuff to keep dis growin' bunch. Besides," and she looks down at her feet sadly, "Sammy's sister, Miss Margaret, died two months ago from de fever. She was only nine, and it grieves dem to stay on. Hannibal is bigger and better anyways."

Sammy jumps up and down, lets out a yell at this and adds with glee, "I'm gonna see me a big river!"

Once again he breaks loose from Jennie and runs to the wagon. His mother lifts him up into the wagon along with the other children. There are Orion, Pamela, and little Benjamin.

Calls of "Good luck, John!" and "Write now, Jane!" come from the neighbors as the wagon moves down the dusty road toward us. Jennie has taken her seat and is holding little Sammy on her lap. As they pass us, she waves; and I hear Sammy say, "I'm gonna see me a big river! That's what I'm gonna do!"

Now, when one pretends to go backwards in time, one must expect surprises. We are astonished to find that by the time we follow the Clemens family to Hannibal, Missouri, five years have passed. It is now the beginning of summer 1845. Sam Clemens is no longer the puny little fellow that waved goodbye to us from the wagon. He is a gangly-legged nine and a half, not tall for his age, but strong and wiry. He has a thick mop of reddish hair which he plasters down to keep it from curling. He has made lots of friends, pulled off more than his share of pranks, and has a reputation for being . . . well, frankly, kind of wild.

Hannibal looks somewhat familiar to us. There are deep woods nearby where boys can hunt opossum and raccoons at night. Holliday Hill on the north side of town can be climbed; and best of all, right in front of the town is a river — the Mississippi — a wide, endless stretch of glistening water, its current swinging to the sea. What a path of adventure, the gateway to the world! One can sit and dream for hours, watching the lazy canoes, the barges and the steamboats that make the river come alive. Of course! Now we recognize it! This is the setting Sam Clemens wrote about much later in *The Adventures of Tom Sawyer!*

Hannibal is a boy's paradise. There are islands with turtles and their eggs, lots of mussels and plenty of fish. There's Bear Creek where the swimming is best and Mac-Dougall's Cave, an underground marvel of deep passages and vaulted chambers that lead into the bluffs and far down into the earth's black silences. There are long corridors hung with stalactites, remote hiding places, a home for bats and a gallant outlaw band or a pirate treasure.

The Clemens home is pointed out to us. We see the white two-storey wooden house with its whitewashed fence on Hill Street. John Clemens has done much better in Hannibal and is a respected judge now. The older boy, Orion, has taken a job in St. Louis in the printing trade. Little Benjamin has died, so there are only three children at home now — Pamela, Sam and little Henry. Let's go knock on the door.

The door is opened by Sam's mother, Jane. She invites us in and treats us to tea as she is eager to talk of her son.

"At first I was afraid Sam was going to die, but now I'm afraid that he isn't! He's such a boy! More trouble than all the other children combined! And what a storyteller he is! I declare, he could make a wooden Indian laugh!" she

says with pride. "Of course, he's always into something. He's the leader of his gang of boys, mostly because he can think of the most outrageous things to do. The Bowen boys and John Briggs and Jim Dunlap are always hanging around here. And, of course, that worthless Tom Blankenship. I do wish he wouldn't play with that one! He's the son of the town drunk, you know. Doesn't have a decent thing to his name, always dirty and barefoot; but Sam likes him best of all."

"Does he like girls at all?" I ask.

"Oh my, yes, indeed! He's kind of sweet on little Laura Hawkins who lives across the street. I saw him give her a rose the other day when he was showing off in front of

her house." She laughs right out loud at this and adds, "Of course, he gave me a present, too. One of those horrid little bats from the caves. Sam loves them and thought I would, too."

She tells us about the time he was brought home half drowned learning to swim. "He drives me crazy with his antics when he's in the house. And when he's out of it, I am expecting every minute that someone will bring him home half dead. I should have known he'd be in no danger from swimming. People born to be hanged are safe in water!"

I can't get over the funny feeling that I am talking to Tom Sawyer's Aunt Polly instead of the real Mrs. Clemens.

We want to catch Sam before he leaves school, so we finish our cake and tea and say goodbye to Mrs. Clemens. By the time we reach the log schoolhouse, the children have disappeared. We do, however, have time to chat with Sam's teacher, a Mrs. Horr.

"That Sam Clemens! He gets into more trouble!" says Mrs. Horr with a sigh. She tells us that Sam had caused a classroom upset last week when he had misbehaved. She had asked him to find her a wooden switch so she could give him a sound licking.

"Do you know what that boy did?" she asks without expecting a reply, "He found a carpenter's shaving curl and brought it to me! The children went into a spasm of laughter!"

"As for studying," Mrs. Horr goes on, "Sam just doesn't

take to school work. Oh, he's good in history and in spelling. He even wins most of the spelling bees; but he spends his time in class gazing out of the window in one of those endless dreams of his, or squirming in his seat, busting to get outside. I really feel for poor Jane Clemens!" Then in a hushed tone she confesses, "He plays hooky, too!"

We have made our excuses and start to back out of the schoolroom when she adds, "If you see that Sam Clemens, tell him to be sure and have his sums right for tomorrow's lesson. Won't do any good, but tell him anyway."

We know it is a hot day; and perhaps, if we will hurry along, we just may catch up with the children down at Bear Creek. As we near the water, we can hear boys' voices talking excitedly about something. When we come into sight, the boys look up and call us to join them. Tom Blankenship, Will Bowen and Sam Clemens are discussing how far it is across the Mississippi to Illinois.

"Oh, about a half a mile, I guess," drawls Tom.

In another few minutes they are talking about swimming, and in another second Sam is boasting loudly that he can swim across. The boys decide that he should. After all, he is the best swimmer, just as he claims to be.

Sam laughs and peels off his clothes. "I'll show you!" he says, "I'll swim to Illinois and back without touching ground!"

Tom Blankenship has taught Sam everything he knows about the river, about the islands, about where to set traps and where to find turtle eggs, as well as how to swim. He slaps him on the back and says to the boys, "Sure, he can do it." But he cautions Sam, "You'd better head upstream going over, Sam. The current is pretty swift."

Sam plunges in and begins his swim to the opposite side of the river.

"Easy does it!" yells Will Bowen.

Sam is taking easy strokes across the river, and we watch him until all we can see is a tiny splash in the water. Tom walks over to us. He is wearing a worn out, faded shirt, no shoes, a battered straw hat, and pants tied at the waist with a rope. Why, he looks like Huckleberry Finn to us.

"He's a devil, he is," says Tom, pointing over his shoulder with his thumb in the direction of Sam's kicking feet. "Him and me, we're like THAT!" and he slaps his hands together firmly. "He has the best ideas for pretendin', and he's willin' to try anythin' once. Last week he told me he was gonna be a riverboat man and travel all the way down to New Orleans. And, you know, I just bet he will, too."

We watch Sam now, a little worried. He has reached the other side and is on his way back. All eyes are on him. Sam has let out a yell. Tom runs to the waterline and shouts, "You okay, Sam?"

Sam doesn't answer. He keeps coming toward us. He doesn't seem to be kicking his feet any longer.

"My glory!" says Will. "He's had a cramp, and he can't move his legs!"

Sam keeps swimming, pulling hard with his arms. He must be hurting bad. At last he is close enough for us to reach him. We drag him in. Gasping and almost unconscious, he lies on the sandy bank. He can't move his legs at all! Tom and Will begin to massage his legs.

"Sam has more nerve than any of us!" says Tom as he moves to one side to let us rub Sam's legs. We have to agree with that!

We know this isn't the time and place to talk with Sam; so we help walk him home to Hill Street, knowing that his mother won't be at all surprised to see him limping up to the door.

The following day, we awake in our hotel room. We glance at the calendar on the wall. It can't be! But it is! It's 1857 already! Sam must be almost twenty-two years old. We'll have to hurry.

In our frantic effort to catch up with him, we find that Sam was only eleven years old when Judge Clemens died, leaving the family strapped for funds. Orion helped out from St. Louis with a little money, Pamela gave music lessons, and Mrs. Clemens took in boarders at the old house on Hill Street. Sam left school at twelve and went to work. We suspect this didn't upset him too much.

Mr. Ament, owner of the Hannibal newspaper called *The Courier*, had given Sam a job as an apprentice, teaching him to set type and run the printing press. In return, Sam promised to work hard, be good, and stay with him for two years.

"He did work hard, too," says Mr. Ament, "and turned out to be a fine printer. Hated to lose him. . . ."

"Where did he go?" we ask.

"Worked a while for his brother, Orion, who tried to start a newspaper here in Hannibal," says Mr. Ament with a frown. "Didn't make it, but they sure tried. Understand the paper failed, and Orion went to Iowa to work on another newspaper. Sam left Hannibal 'fore that time. Laura Hawkins hears from him once in a while. Why don't you ask her?"

We hurry away from the newspaper office and find Laura Hawkins, a pretty young lady who had once been the apple of Sam's eye — maybe still is, for all we know.

Laura, who reminds us of Tom Sawyer's Becky Thatcher, is more than willing to talk of Sam.

"Oh, yes, Sam and Orion worked hard on that old newspaper of theirs. Sam wasn't paid anything much. Orion was cross and cranky and didn't think Sam could write very well. In fact, he said his stories were too dramatic to be believed, but we all loved to read them when Orion would allow them to be printed. I don't think Sam liked working for his brother, but they both tried to make the paper a success. It wasn't though," she says, remembering how Sam looked the day he told her it had failed.

"You know," she smiles as her eyes light up with the telling, "Sam sent some of his stories to a weekly paper in Philadelphia, and they printed them! They didn't pay him any money, but Sam was as happy as a lark!

"He must have showed them to me one hundred times!"

"Where is Sam now?" we ask.

"Oh, he went away!" says Laura. "He left Hannibal to see the world, he said. He's been working in ever so many places! He sent me letters from St. Louis, from New York and Washington; and he worked on *The Inquirer* in Philadelphia, too. Then he went to Iowa to join his brother on the paper there, but I don't think he's there any longer. His last letters have been full of some wild plan to go to South America and make a fortune up the headwaters of the Amazon. That's all I can tell you, except that he may be on his way to Brazil right now!"

We sincerely hope not, for Brazil is so far away. We wonder if we will ever find Sam again. We decide to go down to the river. Perhaps someone, anyone, on board one of the steamboats, will have heard about Sam Clemens. We run along the docks and then hear the familiar cry: "Steamboat's a' comin'." It is a small one called *The Paul Jones* that pulls up alongside the dock. Cargo is being loaded as we make our way to the gang plank and onto the old riverboat with its peeling paint and enormous paddle wheel. Almost immediately the whistle blows, the paddle wheel turns and we are steaming down the Mississippi River. We

HANNIBAL WEEKLY GAZETTE

OUT OF BUSINESS

must find the Captain.

As we climb up the steps to the pilot house, we are met by a crusty old Captain who introduces himself as Captain Horace Bixby, pilot of the *Paul Jones*. When we ask him about Sam Clemens, he puts his head back and roars with laughter.

"Sam Clemens in Brazil!" he shouts. "That's a good one! Come on, I have someone for you to meet!" He leads us to the pilot house. A young man is at the wheel of the ship. He is a rather slender, loose-limbed youth with a fair complexion and a tangle of auburn hair. He is concentrating very hard on the task of steering the riverboat safely down the river.

"Watch that shoreline, Sam, and keep your eyes peeled for stray logs!" he shouts to the young man at the wheel. Then he motions us to join him while he lights up his pipe and tells us, "I'm teachin' the young fellow to be a river pilot. There's your Sam Clemens!" And he laughs once more at our surprised expressions.

"He's learnin' well," says Captain Bixby, puffing on his pipe, "'fore I'm through with him, he'll know every bend and island and sandbar by heart!" Then to Sam, he yells, "Better take a readin' on the depth, Sam," and he goes to the side of the boat, hollering instructions to someone below.

A rope is tossed over the side, and we can hear them yelling back to the pilot house: "Mark three . . . Quarter less three . . . Half twain . . . Quarter twain . . . Mark twain."

"Mark twain . . . we're in safe water now!" says the Captain. Then to Sam he yells, "Okay, you blamed mudcat, keep your eyes peeled!"

"Yep, he takes to the river like a catfish to bait!" says the Captain puffing fiercely on his pipe. "He's a bright lad, and I'm gonna teach him to be the best blamed pilot on the river!"

Now we understand where the writer Sam Clemens found his character Captain Stormfield in *Life On the Mississippi*. We also discover where he found his name, a name that became so well known throughout the world.

That night we sit around the table with the Captain and Sam as they recount stories of their experiences. Sam speaks in a warm, slow way that makes whatever he says sound funny. How we laugh when he tells of his love for cats.

"Cats have a lofty character. They are brave to the point of rashness and almost always unselfish. Why, they give up eight of their lives and reserve only one for themselves," says Sam; then adds, "Cats are packed full of music . . . just as full as they can hold. And when they die, people remove it from them and sell it to the fiddlemakers!"

We fall on our bunks that night exhausted from laughing so much.

It is startling to find that, when we awake the next morning, we are no longer aboard the *Paul Jones*! We look

around in alarm at our new quarters. We aren't on board a ship! We are in a hotel room, and the morning paper is dated June 16, 1865!

We hear a wagon roll underneath our window and rush to look out. We've been whisked by some magic to the West and into the most flourishing mining town in Nevada, a town called Virginia City. A man named Comstock had discovered a rich vein of silver ore about three years ago. Miners, speculators and adventurers swarmed into the town from everywhere. What a spot for a young man! Sam must be here. Let's see, he's almost thirty years old now.

We ask the desk clerk where we can get some information; and he directs us to the office of the town's leading newspaper, *The Enterprise.*

"Sam Clemens? Clemens? Oh, that would be Mark . . . Mark Twain, our reporter. He's out right now. Can I be of help? The name's Dan . . . Dan de Quille," says a young man, reaching across his desk to shake my hand.

We learn from Dan that Sam's career as a riverboat captain had come to a sudden end at the outbreak of the Civil War. He and his brother, Orion, had come West. Orion had a job as assistant to the governor of the Nevada Territory, and Sam had been bitten with gold fever, had headed for the hills to dig along with hundreds of other miners.

He had made a lot of friends, swapped stories in his Southern drawl, and sent some of his letters to different newspapers around the country. He never got rich digging for gold, for all the rocks he collected proved to be worthless. He then took a job in a quartz mill, separating silver from ore, and worked from dawn till dusk, but never learned how properly to handle the shovel. He was fired.

One day he got a letter that offered him a job on *The Enterprise* for $25 a month; and he walked all the way from the mine fields, dirt and all, to become a reporter.

"We have a lot to write about out here. Men get rich overnight. There's shootin's and killin's almost daily. Sam started signing 'Mark Twain' to his work 'bout two years ago; and . . . well, it just stuck. We call him Mark now . . . most people do. Wouldn't know who Sam Clemens was if you asked," says Dan. "Say, did you hear about how Mark got a story published in a big magazine in New York? It was one he heard around the minin' camp 'bout a jumpin' contest between two frogs."

"Yes," I say a little too smugly. "Everyone knows *The Celebrated Jumping Frog of Calaveras County.*"

"They do, huh? Well, it's a good yarn, and Mark's happy 'bout the money it's been makin'," says Dan, not aware of my slip. "Mark's been invited to go to San Francisco by that lecture fella, Artemus Ward. The old man says he can make a speaker out of him. Mark even grew a mustache. Thought it would look more dignified, he said. Can you imagine, Mark Twain as a speaker!"

"Yes, I think I can," I say with a smile.

Dan glances at his pocket watch and says, "You just might catch Mark now. He's probably swappin' lies at the Bucket of Blood Saloon down the street. 'Course, if you can stay over till tomorrow . . . ."

We say a hurried goodbye and leave the *Enterprise* office, knowing that tomorrow, for us, might be years from now.

We can hear the music of a tinkling piano, the sound of laughter and shouts of men's voices as we near the entrance of the saloon. A couple of unshaven men in tight fitting britches with guns on their hips push past us. With their spurs and boots they clomp across the wooden boardwalk and disappear through the swinging doors of the barroom.

We look at each other, a little frightened, yet keep walking toward the saloon. We push the swinging door and step inside. Suddenly the noise has stopped, and we are in total blackness. The air smells heavy and damp. Slowly we grope along the walls of what seems to be an endless tunnel, turning and twisting until we see a light in the distance. We run toward it. It gets brighter and brighter. At last we step out of this mysterious tunnel of darkness into Hartford, Connecticut, in the year 1882.

A little girl in a white pinafore is watching us. We rub our eyes and look around in bewildered amazement to find that time has raced ahead 17 years. The child waves to us and tells us that her name is Susy . . . Susy Clemens. This

must be Mark Twain's daughter, and we didn't even know he was married!

We run after Susy who leads us toward the oddest-looking house we have ever seen . . . turrets, balconies, a huge veranda, and a forest of chimneys. Why, it looks part steamboat, part medieval castle, and part cuckoo clock!

"That's Nook Farm!" Susy informs us. "Papa designed it so we could watch parades and circuses go by!"

Another girl, slightly smaller than Susy, waves to us from one of the balconies and soon joins us, dragging along a fat two-year-old. We are introduced to Clara and Jean, the baby.

"Come on!" says Susy, guiding us inside to a comfortable room. Here we see shelves of books along two walls and a huge fireplace with a big mantelpiece crowded with bric-a-brac. A crackling fire warms the room. It's a happy place.

"How nice of you to come to see us!" says a soft voice. We turn around and see a lovely lady, her arms full of cut roses. As she arranges them in a vase, she speaks again, "I'm Olivia Clemens, but you can call me Livy. Please, make yourself comfortable. Youth will join us in a minute. He's upstairs putting the finishing touches on a new book of his called *Huckleberry Finn.*"

Once we were settled, Mrs. Clemens tells us of their marriage and how successful things had been for them with 'Youth's' wonderful books. "We have a happy, lovely time," she explains, "and Sam is so good with the children. He loves children . . . all children . . . and they love him back." We can feel the happiness in this room and know it is true.

"It was a little difficult getting used to Sam. He's not like other people, you know. He's liable to do and say anything! Just yesterday he found a shirt without a button on it in his drawer, and he took every single shirt out of that drawer and threw it out the window!" She laughs as she speaks.

Just then our attention turns to the doorway. There stands Mark Twain leaning against the door jamb, hands over his chest, smiling a warm, happy grin as he listens to our conversation.

"Flattery will get you someplace, Livy. That should be a lesson to me. Never do wrong when someone is looking," he says in his familiar drawl. Then changing the subject quickly, he says, "I've just looked in the hothouse, my dear, and there is a perfect world of flowers in bloom. Too bad we haven't a corpse!"

We laugh; and he joins us, his eyes twinkling with merriment.

"Oh Papa! Can we play horse?" says Susy, running to her father.

"All right," he says. "We'll play horse or anything you like."

He gets down on his knees, and the children climb on his back and pull his hair as he romps around on all fours. Then he sings some hymns, acting them out as he sings.

He plays the piano, too; but he really isn't very good at it, and the sour notes make us giggle.

He tells us some stories; and when it is time for the children to be tucked into bed, he kisses them all soundly and pats their backsides, before Livy takes them off to their room.

"I swear," he says, sighing with content, "if all of my days are as happy as these, I deliberately fooled away thirty years of my life before I got married! If I were to do it over again, I would marry in early infancy instead of wasting time cutting teeth and breaking things."

Taking a cigar out of his waistcoat pocket, he bites off the end, wets it, lights it, and closes his eyes, enjoying the sweet aroma of the smoke. I cough. Immediately he takes the cigar out of his mouth and points it in my direction.

"Sorry if it bothers you. You know, I make it a point never to smoke more than one cigar at a time." He continues to puff away.

We explain how we have come from another century and how we have been walking in his footsteps; for in our century his books are classics of children's literature.

"Classics!" He booms with laughter, "Bah! My books are water! Those classics of the great geniuses are wine!" Then with a twinkle in his eye he adds, "Of course, everybody drinks water!"

We tell him how he will travel to Europe and become even more famous, how big universities will give him honorary degrees, how he will be known as the most "American" of authors and how his universal wit and humor will win the love of all the world.

He blushes a little at all this, puffs on his cigar thoughtfully, then answers, "You know, I've had compliments many times, and it always embarrasses me. I always feel that they have never said enough."

With those words ringing in our ears, we leave the happiness of the Clemens home, knowing that our journey has somehow come to a close.

It is no surprise to find that we are walking down our own street, and the year is now. We know that Sam lived to be seventy-four years old; and that when Halley's Comet once again lit the midnight sky in April, 1910, Mark Twain closed his eyes for the last time. He had been born with a matchless gift of words, and his whole life had developed it to a rare perfection.

We turned in our story to our editor the next day, but let me ask you something. Did you hear what I heard when we left the editor's desk? I could have sworn I heard a whisper. It was a soft Southern drawl, and it said, "Yep, like I said, they never say enough!"

Ginny Benson

In the first stanza of a thirty-year career in writing, Ginny Benson worked as a feature writer for Associated Press in South America. This experience was a springboard to advertising in New York, sales promotion in Florida and publicity in Washington, D.C. She has been a columnist/sports writer in the South.

She returned to her native California in 1963, opening up her own advertising and public relations firm until 1972 when she found, much to her surprise, that writing for children was the happiest thing she had ever done. She has had over 175 stories published since that time in audio visuals, remedial reading programs, and poetry in children's magazines. She has served as consultant to the Times-Mirror Early Exploration Program for pre-school children.

With this first book under her belt, she is again hard at work on a second novel for children.

Harold Henriksen

Harold Henriksen was born in St. Paul, Minnesota, and has lived there most of his life. He attended the School of the Associated Arts in St. Paul.

Even while serving in the Army, Harold continued to keep alive his desire to become an artist. In 1965 he was a winner in the All Army Art Contest.

After the Army, Harold returned to Minnesota where he worked for several art studios in the Minneapolis-St. Paul area. In 1967 he became an illustrator for one of the largest art studios in Minneapolis.

During 1971 Harold and his wife traveled to South America where he did on-the-spot drawings for a year. Harold, his wife, and his daughter Maria now live in Minneapolis where he works as a free lance illustrator.

Walt Disney
Bob Hope
Duke Ellington
Dwight Eisenhower
Coretta King
Pablo Picasso
Ralph Nader
Bill Cosby
Dag Hammarskjold
Sir Frederick Banting
Mark Twain
Beatrix Potter

**close
ups**